Semi Trucks of the 1960s

Ron Adams

Iconografix

Iconografix
1830A Hanley Road
Hudson, Wisconsin 54016 USA

Library of Congress Control Number: 2012935604

ISBN-13: 978-1-58388-300-6
ISBN-10: 1-58388-300-2

Printed in The United States of America

Book Proposals

Iconografix is a publishing company specializing in books for transportation enthusiasts. We publish in a number of different areas, including Automobiles, Auto Racing, Buses, Construction Equipment, Emergency Equipment, Farming Equipment, Railroads & Trucks. The Iconografix imprint is constantly growing and expanding into new subject areas.

Authors, editors, and knowledgeable enthusiasts in the field of transportation history are invited to contact the Editorial Department at Iconografix, 1830A Hanley Rd., Hudson, WI 54016.

Dedication

Shortly after graduating from high school in 1965, I worked hard and saved up to purchase my first car and my first Polaroid camera. I would go to a spot along Route 22 (or I-78) and take pictures of trucks traveling along the highway. On March 20, 1966 I was almost ready to leave to go and do some picture taking when there was a knock on the front door. My brother called me to the door and the man held his hand out to shake hands and introduce himself as Joe Wanchura. He told me that he saw some of my truck pictures in *Overdrive* magazine in their tractor-of-the-month contest and decided to look me up.

I invited him in and then we started talking trucks. I didn't know too much about trucks at that time to keep up with him but somehow we managed to talk trucks for most of the day. We went out to the street where his truck was parked, a 1964 DCO-405 International Emeryville. He got his pictures out of his truck and also a model of his truck that he was building from scratch. We took these things back to my home and started looking through his black and white pictures that he took in the 1940s in Chicago. They were an awesome sight to see, as was the model he was working on. He mentioned that he drove for Hayes Freight Lines and then Pirkle Refrigerated Freight Lines of Cudahy, Wisconsin, and we spent the rest of the day swapping stories. Before he left, he gave to me about 10 of his older pictures, one of them being a 1936 Dieselized C Model International sleeper that pulled for Cooper-Jarrett Motor Freight.

The next day at work I could not stop thinking about what happened the day before. We continued to trade photographs over the next many years. He has a great collection of the kind of truck pictures that everyone loves to see. When I look through my truck pictures and I come across some that he took, it takes me back in memory to that Sunday afternoon in March of 1966, the day I got to meet a great and knowledgeable man. Since this book is about the 1960s and it was near the middle of the decade that we met, Joe, this one is for you!

Introduction

For trucking companies, the decade of the Fifties was a tumultuous time with many buyouts and mergers taking place. Pacific Intermountain Express Inc. (P.I.E.) took over the operations of West Coast Fast Freight. Spector Motor Service Inc. took over Mid-States Freight Lines. Johnson Motor Line Inc. took over Atlantic States Motor Lines Inc, Norwalk Truck Lines Inc. took over Shirks Motor Express Inc., Ringsby Truck Lines Inc. took over Inland Freight Lines Inc. Strickland Transportation Co. took over Kelleher Motor Freight Lines, and Emery Transportation Co. merged with Midwest Freight Co. and became Midwest-Emery Freight System Inc. There were more buyouts and mergers that occurred but these were just a few.

The buyouts and mergers gave these companies the opportunity to serve more customers and expand their operations into new territories. To give an example, Strickland Transportation's operating territory had been Texas, Oklahoma, Arkansas, Missouri and Illinois. After the purchase of Kelleher their operating territory expanded from Illinois on into the mid-Atlantic and New England states.

Not only did the trucking companies go through changes but so did the truck manufacturers. For instance, White Motor Co. took over four manufacturers—Sterling, Autocar, Reo and Diamond T, with Sterling being the one to become lost to history. Several of the manufacturers started to offer a bigger variety of the existing models and introduced some new ones. The "B" model Mack that was introduced in 1953 replaced the "L" series. Mack's "N" low cab-over-engine model made its debut, and the "G" model came in 1958. Mack also

restyled the "H" series at the end of the decade. International put together a line-up of a number of different and new models like the R, V, CO, VCO, BC, and the famous DCO 405 Emeryville. These are just two of the manufacturers that expanded their model lines. What all this meant is that the customer had a wider choice to suit the individual's needs for the truck to fit the right job.

Also, at the end of the Fifties, 40-foot trailers were becoming a reality so the manufacturers had to design short wheelbase tractors to pull these trailers and stay within the 50-foot legal length limit in many states.

So by the end of the Fifties there was a much wider selection of models. Although many models were carry-overs from the Fifties, there were many more different makes and models of trucks through the Sixties: Autocar's DC and A series (which was all-aluminum); Brockway's 200, 300 and 400 series; Diamond T's short wheelbase 990 and 931 C (that got a face lift and became the CO series). Also, the new-born Diamond Reo. Ford made their contribution with the new "N" series conventional and the totally new H series cab-over-engine which was very muscular looking, especially the sleeper cab version. This was later replaced with the "W" series cab-over-engines. White-Freightliner introduced a first in the industry which was the all-new 104-inch cab known as the "Vanliner." GMC started producing their "cracker box" D series which was later replaced with the Astro 95. GMC also came on strong with the 9500 long nose and short nose models. International had a lot of the Fifties models coming into the Sixties. They also introduced new models like the "D-400" series which replaced the RD 300 and 400 models. A host of "stars" were also in the line-up. The very famous Emeryville was replaced in 1965 with the CO-4000, which later became the Transtar. Kenworth improved and made some restyling changes to their "K" line and "W" series. A lot of the Mack models also came over to the Sixties, especially their famous B model. Then came the F series in 1962, the F series Mack Western in 1964, and the R series in 1966 along with the R Series Mack Western. Also introduced was the new DM series "dump and mixer." Peterbilt came on the scene in 1967 with an all-new big hit, the 359 Conventional with the big 1,444-square-inch radiator. In 1968, there was the model 352 that got a little facelift and was known as the Pacemaker. White had their new 3000, 4000, 5000, and then the replacement for the 5000 which was the 7000. Also in 1968, a new star was born which was named White Western Star, which was the beefed-up version of the 4000 model. There were a great number more so these are just a briefing.

The Sixties was the decade for expansion, not only for the truck manufacturers with a huge selection of models, but also for the trucking companies themselves. By purchasing carriers that met at their connecting points, more companies were able to provide coast-to-coast service. Denver-Chicago Trucking Co. in Denver, Colorado, held the honor for many years of being the first coast-to-coast carrier since 1946. It is interesting to note that it was mainly the western trucking companies taking over the eastern companies. In 1960, Consolidated Freightways of Menlo Park, California, took over Motor Cargo Co. of Akron, Ohio. Navajo Freight Lines Inc. of Denver, Colorado, took over General Expressways of Chicago, Illinois.

General Express became the new name of the reorganization of Keeshin Freight System. In the year of 1962 Watson Bros. Transportation Co. of Omaha, Nebraska, took over the Wilson Truck Co. of Nashville, Tennessee, and T.I.M.E. Freight Inc. of Lubbock, Texas, took over Super Service Motor Freight also of Nashville, Tennessee. Around 1965, Transcon Lines Inc. of El Segundo, California, took over Kramer-Consolidated Fright Lines of Detroit, Michigan. The year 1966 was when Pacific Intermountain Express of Oakland, California, finally accomplished what they had tried to do in the early Fifties (go coast to coast), by the purchase of All States Freight in Akron, Ohio, and IML Freight Inc., in Salt Lake City, Utah, with their purchase of Eastern Motor Dispatch in Columbus, Ohio.

Other mergers were also taking place like Eastern Express and Wheelock Bros., Lee Way Motor Freight and Texas-Arizona Motor Freight, Western Truck Lines and Gillette Motor Transport, McLean Trucking and Hayes Freight Lines, Mason-Dixon Lines and Silver Fleet Motor Express, Smith Transfer and Huber & Huber Motor Express, United Truck Lines and Buckingham Transportation Co., Adley Express and Miller Motor Express just to mention a few. And in 1969, three giant carriers merged into one—Denver-Chicago Trucking Co., Time Freight Inc., and Los Angeles-Seattle Motor Express became Time-DC.

You might say that the Fifties was an aggressive decade, but the Sixties seemed to take it one step further. Yet, the mergers and buyouts opened the door for better and faster service coast to coast, expanding the availability of products throughout the country.

The Autocar was a beast of a truck. This DC103645-OH was powered by a 190-horsepower Cummins Diesel engine with a 5x3 transmission that ran on 11:00-24 tires. With three-speed auxiliary transmission, this truck's sturdiness and toughness qualified it to do all kinds of grueling jobs. Here it is being loaded with 15 1/2 yards of sulfur. The stretch is a 177-inch wheelbase. A few extra items and a chrome radiator shell give this truck a great appearance. Carmen Yannuzzi & Sons of Belleville, New Jersey, are the proud owners. *Autocar Trucks*

The American Thread Co. of Bristol, Tennessee, decided to use this H-67 Mack as the power source to pull the Black Diamond model A5-7740 straight-floor 40-foot trailer. Notice that the grille on this model is the same grille used on the G-73 model. *Black Diamond Inc.*

Double 40-foot trailers, or turnpike trains, were coming on strong in the early Sixties. One of the companies that ran these doubles was Keeshin Freight System Inc. This G-73 Mack was leased to Keeshin and on this job pulled a Highway and Fruehauf trailer combination. These trains could be seen on the Massachusetts pike, Ohio and Indiana turnpikes and the New York state thruway. *Neil Sherff*

"Texas-bred, Texas-fed beef, none better anywhere" was the slogan for the Texas Meat Packers Inc. of Dallas, Texas. They used this Kenworth cab-over-engine tractor to haul their products in the reefer trailer. The tractor is powered by a Cummins Diesel. *Author's Collection*

This model 351 Peterbilt was kept busy hauling fans, transformers and other electrical components on a special-built flatbed trailer. Although there is no identification, it is possible that this rig was used in the fleet of the City of Los Angeles. *Peterbilt Motor Co.*

A popular western combination was the truck-trailer rig. Mitchell Bros. of Portland, Oregon, owned this Kenworth with flat body trailer that was used to haul rolled cable on this trip. Mitchell Bros. served the states of California, Oregon, Washington, and Idaho. This is one of several different types of rigs in their fleet. *Ackroyd Photography*

Maybe feeling a little out of place compared to its two neighbors on the right is this DC-75 Autocar owned by John Suttles of Taylor, South Carolina. The Autocars always had that tough looking, hard working appearance. Suttles was contracted to H&M Motor Lines of Greenville, South Carolina. *Harry Patterson*

The B-model Macks and Great Dane trailers were a very popular team with a lot of southern produce haulers. Most of the trucks had integral, or factory, sleeper cabs, but in this case the owner chose an add-on box sleeper. This Florida-based B-61 Mack is a simple truck that got the job done well. *Author's Collection*

Brockway trucks, one of two 'dog' brand trucks made in the East, were known as the "Huskies." These three model N-260s were in the Tayntons fleet based in Wellsboro, Pennsylvania, and served thirteen New England and Midwest states. Fruehauf trailers were teamed up with the model N-260s. *Tom Gill's Photo*

Another southern produce hauler combination is again a Mack and Great Dane reefer trailer. This B-73 model has the Charlotte sleeper with the comforts of an air conditioner for its owner and driver Charles Boswell. The company he leased to is unknown. *Author's Collection*

A rare sight in Iowa was this truck-trailer combination. This Kenworth had a Winger Bulkmaster body with the same brand name trailer. A rig like this one was probably used for hauling scrap metal. *Kenworth Truck Co.*

The RD-400 series was the big western-style model for International. In 1961, production of this model was discontinued and was replaced by the new "D" series. The one we see here was owned by Nevada Sales & Service of Las Vegas, Nevada. The driver had the comforts of an add-on sleeper box that was kept cool by a cab-mounted air conditioner. The merchandise being shipped was also kept cool in the Utility reefer trailer. *Brian Williams*

What looks like a new truck is actually only a repainted older truck. This model 351 cab-over-engine, that is pulling a Fruehauf grain trailer, got its facelift at Woodpecker Truck & Equipment Co. in Pendleton, Oregon. Notice the Woodpecker on the right front corner of the cab. *Woodpecker Truck and Equipment Co.*

In late 1960, Ford entered the high cab-over-engine field with their new "H" series. It was their first Diesel-powered line hauler. The HD-950 and the HD-1000 were available in either tandem or single axle and also with or without a sleeper cab. A popular engine for this series was the NH-220 Cummins Diesel. *Ford Motor Co.*

Based in Bridgeport, Connecticut, Middle Atlantic Transportation Co. Inc. covered territory from Connecticut to Michigan. One of the tractors in the famous blue and white fleet was this H-67 Mack. The H-67 was produced from 1958 to 1962. Notice that the saddle fuel tanks look like it could be a homemade one instead of a vendor's tank. *Neil Sherff*

Based in Illinois, Central and Southern Truck Lines Inc.'s fleet was made up of a variety of various makes. One of those makes was this White model 5000 that pulled a Fruehauf reefer trailer and was owned by F. & J. Ely. The 5000 model was White's first high cab-over-engine model. *Neil Sherff*

"Round 'em up, Load 'em up and Haul 'em out"—that was the job for El Paso Livestock Express Inc. Based in El Paso, Texas, their tractors were Kenworths that pulled Wilson possum-belly livestock trailers. The Southwest was the main scope of their operations. *El Paso Livestock Express*

This 921-F Diamond T was sitting idle, waiting for a load to go. The factory sleeper model was on lease with Daniel's Motor Freight Inc. of Warren, Ohio. It covered an area from Chicago to New England as it hauled steel and general commodities. In 1968, Daniels Motor Freight Inc. seized operations after being taken over by Eazor Express Inc. of Pittsburgh, Pennsylvania. *Neil Sherff*

M&H Produce Inc. of Fort Worth, Texas, took to the road in this circa-1960 International DCOF-405 Emeryville and Lufkin reefer trailer. With dual air horns, a sun visor, a chrome stack on the 80-inch cab, and white spoke wheels, it made for a rather impressive looking rig as it traveled through the Southwest and West. *Author's Collection*

Travelers in the states of Minnesota, Wisconsin and Illinois could view the trucks that carried the Indian graphics for Chippewa Motor Freight Inc. of Eau Claire, Wisconsin. The company hauled general commodities and offered heated and refrigerated services. One of the rigs that took part in the action was this B-61 Mack and Trailmobile reefer trailer. *Chippewa Motor Freight Inc.*

The White model 5000 was a rather popular truck, not only with the trucking companies but with the private carriers as well. In this case the private carrier is Burlington Industries Inc. based in Burlington, North Carolina. A Great Dane trailer is the cargo partner to the tractor. *Author's Collection*

From the Pacific Coast, through the Rocky Mountains and over the Great Plains into Chicago was the area where the trucks for Pacific Intermountain Express Inc. of Oakland, California, were seen. This model 351 Peterbilt cab-over-engine was one of many Peterbilts in the P-I-E fleet, along with this Fruehauf reefer trailer. P-I-E had a large fleet of trucks and did a large volume of business and was always among the top five carriers in the nation. *Neil Sherff*

According to the big number one on front of this tractor, Moe Trucking Co. of Dickinson, North Dakota, must have just started in the livestock hauling business. The two unknown drivers are standing happy and proud beside their White-Freightliner tractor and new Wilson possum-belly livestock trailer. Livestock hauling was big business for the Great Plains area. *Woodworth Photography*

The White Mustang was a good, all-around truck to do almost any job. In this case it was in the construction industry as a mixer truck. The owner was Warner Sand, Gravel and Lime Products. Warner could possibly be the oldest existing trucking business because on the door decal it mentions Warner was founded in the year 1794. *White Motor Co.*

Not all trucks that came up from the South and Southwest were tractor-trailers. In this case we have a B-61 Mack for Russell Produce Co., based in McAllen, Texas. The produce was kept cool in the reefer body by the Thermo King refrigeration unit. Notice the walking rack over the top of the cab. *Harry Patterson*

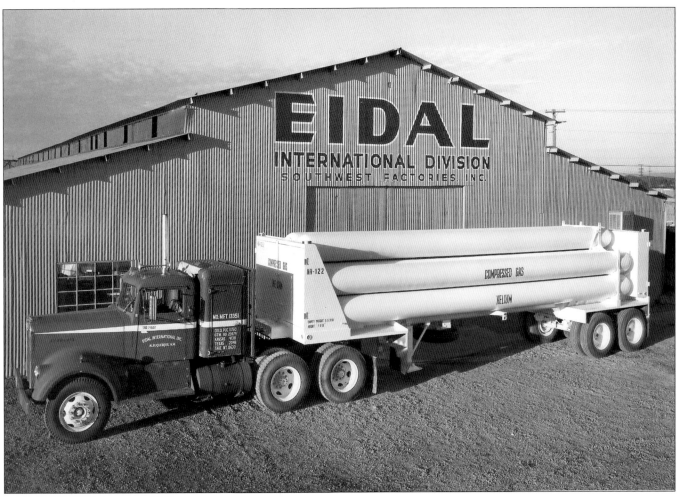

Eidal International Inc. was a manufacturer of specialized tank trailers such as the one we see here to transport helium. Eidal's location was Albuquerque, New Mexico. The tractor is a Kenworth that is on lease from Ryder Rentals. On this short wheelbase tractor they still found room to squeeze in a sleeper box and headache rack. *Dick Kent Photography*

The White 5000 models made their way into all different kinds of hauling in the trucking field. This Wilson open-top livestock trailer served for an unknown hauler from Iowa. The 5000 model came in single axle form or they were also available with tandem axles. *Neil Sherff*

Harry Frost of St. Paul, Minnesota, and Sioux City, Iowa, had his 931C Diamond T leased to Chatsworth Co-op of Chatsworth, Illinois, here with a mid-1950s era Fruehauf trailer. There was not anything fancy about this rig but Mr. Frost felt that he didn't need all those extra fancy items and was satisfied with a plain-jane truck. *Harry Patterson*

When you look at this tractor you get the feeling that all eyes are upon you with all those headlights. This tractor is a Hendrickson, modified with a CO model International cab. Hendrickson made quite a number of trucks using several other manufacturer's cabs. Southern Express Co. had this one pull an open-top trailer. The muffler looks similar to what Diamond T used. *Neil Sherff*

In the West, many loads of lumber were hauled on flat bed truck-trailer combinations like this one. One of the many companies that hauled these kinds of loads was G&O Hauling based in Pico Rivera, California. The truck body and load were on a White-Freightliner truck. *Author's Collection*

Diamond Ts were offered with the front axle back or forward and either with the chrome bars or the aluminum radiator. The one seen here is a 921F (axle forward) with the aluminum radiator. The trailer is a Brown. The rig is owned by T.W. Burleson's & Son of Waxahachie, Texas. Honey is the commodity being hauled. *Diamond T*

The G-73 model Mack could be seen in all parts of the country and in different trucking operations. D.O. Jackson of Lynnwood, Washington, ran in the eastern states with his Aero-Liner reefer trailer that hauled refrigerated products. The "G" model was produced from 1958 to 1962 with over 2,100 produced. *Neil Sherff*

A lot of Florida fruits and produce came to the northern markets by truck. One of the companies that hauled these commodities was Greenstein Trucking Co. based in Pompano Beach, Florida. A variety of different brand name trucks made up the fleet. One of those trucks was this H-950 Ford with a Fruehauf reefer trailer. The driver had the comfort of a sleeper cab. The tractor was powered by a Caterpillar Diesel. *Neil Sherff*

In 1962 I sent a roll of film to Albuquerque-Phoenix Express in Albuquerque, New Mexico, asking them if they would take some pictures of their trucks for me. They granted my request and this is one of them. The Kenworth dromedary tractor is taking a trailer to the dock to be loaded. The driver was kept cool with the aid of an air conditioner while traveling "the sunshine routes of the great Southwest." *Apex*

Another photo I received form Albuquerque-Phoenix Express Inc. was this postcard. This Kenworth cab-over-engine tractor, powered by a 335-horsepower Cummins Diesel, was photographed pulling a set of 27-foot Fruehauf trailers through the Arizona deserts. These rigs made overnight runs between Phoenix and Albuquerque. *Apex*

Little Audrey's Transportation Co. Inc. of Fremont, Nebraska, Hauled refrigerated products from the Midwest to the Pacific Coast. The fleet consisted of many owner-operators who owned various makes of trucks. In this case it was a model 931-C Diamond T with a Fruehauf reefer trailer. Long wheelbase tractors like this one were legal in the western states. *Neil Sherff*

The "G" model Mack was a great cab-over-engine tractor. This G73 was teamed up with a Lufkin reefer trailer which could be owned by someone in Texas. Notice how Mack was ahead of its rivals with the placement of the door handle. Other manufacturers did not follow this change until about 10 years later. *Author's Collection*

The Coors Brewing Co. in Golden, Colorado, had several contract carriers hauling their brew throughout the West. All of the carriers had the colors of black and red. This custom Kenworth surely drew a lot of attention as it went down the highway pulling the Brown reefer trailer. *Neil Sherff*

Brockways were not only used as over-the-road trucks but they also served their tour of duty in the military. The U.S. Air Force chose this long wheelbase tractor, possibly a model 260, for their over-the-road work. The specification sheets show that the longest available wheelbase was 207 inches. This rig was most likely used in the western states. *Brockway Trucks*

Wilson Freight Forwarding Co., based in Cincinnati, Ohio, was one of the large carriers. The Wilson fleet utilized mostly Macks and Whites. Pictured here is a B-67 Mack, which had the concave cab, pulling a Gindy trailer. Wilson served an area from the Midwest to the East Coast, using about 400 tractors and equally as many trailers. *Wilson Freight Co.*

Hogue Steel Express Inc., based in Michigan, was strictly in the steel hauling business. The state of Michigan allowed several different axle configurations, up to as many as thirteen axles. This setup here shows ten. The short wheelbase tractor is a Diamond T model 990. *Neil Sherff*

Glenwood Springs, Colorado, was the home of the L-P Gas and Appliance Co., who hauled compressed fuel in this Kenworth tractor with a Lubbock tank trailer. Long wheelbase tractors were a common sight in Colorado. *Author's Collection*

Inviting you to "Eat Out More Often" is the S.E. Rykoff & Co., food-service specialists for your favorite restaurants. On this day the products were delivered in a White-Freightliner tractor and a Fruehauf trailer. The colors of the Rykoff trucks were bright green with dark green. *Michael Y'Barra Photography*

The Pacific Molasses Co. of San Francisco, California, had four terminals based throughout the state—Wilmington, Richmond, San Diego, and Stockton. They were a contract carrier for all dry and bulk liquids except petroleum products. One of the rigs that traveled between these terminals was this Kenworth with a set of bottom hopper tank trailers of an unknown brand. *Author's Collection*

Here we have another Kenworth, but this time in the form of a truck-trailer tanker. Pacific Molasses Co. is the owner of the rig. This one was based in Richmond, California. *Brian Williams*

Looking you right in the eye is this big DC-75 Autocar that is at this time pulling an empty Fruehauf reefer trailer. The driver of this load for Hygrade Food Products of Detroit, Michigan, is waiting for a return load. A second bumper was added along with the safety stripes. Notice the Michigan-style pin striping and also the chrome hubcap on the front wheel. *Neil Sherff*

A model 352 Peterbilt stands proudly at the unloading dock at the produce center in Philadelphia. Miles Trucking Co. of Plant City, Florida, owns the tractor and the Gindy trailer. Many southern produce haulers made their way to the produce terminal to deliver fresh southern produce. The picture was taken on July 17, 1966. *Robert Parrish*

Diamond T trucks fit well with almost every operation where trucks could be used. The construction industry was no exception. Here we see a load of cement blocks being delivered to a job site by a model 990-50M-OH. The deliverer was Concrete Specialists Co. in Lyndhurst, New Jersey. *Diamond T*

Back in these times, cars were much bigger than they are today. Most full-size cars today are even smaller than a compact car of this time, such as the Ford Falcon. Four big cars and two compact cars make up this load that is being hauled on a Troyler trailer pulled by a 700 series Dodge tractor. The trailer length is 37-1/2 feet, the overall length is 50 feet and the height is 13 feet, 6 inches. *Troyler Corp.*

By the early Sixties, Kenworths were starting to make their way to the eastern states. One of those Kenworths was owned by Western Distributing Co. of Denver, Colorado, here with an early-Fifties Fruehauf trailer. These stainless steel trailers were very popular with many carriers. *Neil Sherff*

One of the bigger reefer haulers in the South was Belford Trucking Co. of Miami, Florida. This V-6 GMC, pulling a reefer trailer, was one of many different tractors that made up the fleet. Belford covered most of the eastern half of the United States and was one of the four refrigerated carriers owned by Midwest Emery Freight System Inc. of Chicago, Illinois. *Neil Sherff*

As mentioned earlier, Kenworths were making their way east by the early Sixties. Most of them were cab-over-engines because of the length laws. One of those cab-over-engines was this one owned by Airport Machinery Corp. that pulled a West Coast rackside trailer. The driver kept cool by the courtesy of an air conditioner. *Robert Parrish*

Loaded and ready to haul is this model 351 Peterbilt. The body and the transfer dump trailer were both made by Timpte. After being unloaded, the trailer will then be transferred into the truck body on the return trip. *Timpte Inc.*

Although seen at a later date, this early Sixties long wheelbase Kenworth with a reefer trailer included one or two modern day items like the Texas size bumper. These were the first fiberglass tilt hoods that Kenworth made. *Rick Manz*

Produce out of Texas was shipped nationwide. This load was delivered somewhere in Michigan. The job was done by Ledesma Brothers Produce Co. of Carrizo Springs, Texas, with tractor No. 6. The power source is an HD-950 Ford Diesel with a sleeper cab. Many of the produce trailers from the Fifties had the little putt-putt motors. *Neil Sherff*

Again, here's another rig out of Texas. One of the most famous cab-over-engines was this DCOF-405 International Emeryville with a Trailmobile reefer trailer. The rig was leased to the Milk House Cheese Corp. of San Antonio, Texas. The owner selected the 80-inch sleeper cab. The Emeryville cabs had about the biggest windshield of all cab-over-engine cabs. Notice all the license plates on the bumper and all the permit numbers printed on the cab. These were required at the time. *Neil Sherff*

The G-73 Mack was a handsome-looking tractor. Its appearance was similar to the Kenworth cab-over-engine. It had a large windshield which made for better vision. Coast-to-Coast Truck Rentals owned this tractor and Pike trailer. *Author's Collection*

Double trailers have been a big hit in the West almost since the beginning of trucking. Double trailers came in all types. Here we see a set of double Timpte bottom hopper grain trailers. They are being pulled by a Kenworth. The rig is owned by S&V Trucking Co. of Albuquerque, New Mexico, serving the southwestern states. *Timpte Inc.*

Mistletoe Express of Oklahoma City, Oklahoma, was mainly an air express package carrier. They served the whole state of Oklahoma and also northern Texas. The Reo tractor, which is running on propane, is pulling a Morgan trailer. Notice that this trailer has the undercarriage chassis. *Mistletoe Express*

As a kid, playing in the dirt and getting dirty was a lot of fun. In this case, playing in the dirt was serious business for this Mack M45 SX off-highway dump truck. Many tons of earth can be moved in one day by this big dog. *Mack Trucks*

Kenworth Trucks have always had great looking color schemes and paint designs. This tractor is no exception. Grant Produce of Winchester, Tennessee, felt proud of "Voo Doo" all fancied up in its Sunday best. All the chrome extras and dual stacks treat the eye to a sharp looking tractor. *Neil Sherff*

Reefer haulers were many at this time. Among the scene was Little Audrey's Transportation Co. Inc. of Fremont, Nebraska. Owner-operators made up the bulk of the fleet. One of the stars of the show was this 931F Diamond T. With long hauls from the Midwest to the Pacific Coast, a sleeper box was added for those resting times. This owner-driver had his truck painted the company colors of blue and silver. Little Audry's was one of four companies that was owned by Midwest Emery Freight System based in Chicago, Illinois. *Neil Sherff*

This Kenworth was a truck that ran in the western states. It was owned by Kenneth Lynch of Salt Lake City, Utah, and Fresno, California. In the mid-Sixties he started running coast-to-coast. Produce and refrigerated commodities were the loads. *Author's Collection*

This 1962 DCO-405 International Emeryville was owned by none other than Mr. Joe Wanchura of Muncie, Indiana. He was leased on with U.S.A.C. Transport Inc. of Detroit, Michigan. Joe put on a lot of miles running cross-country hauling a lot of government loads. On this trip the load was on a Fruehauf trailer. Notice how nice and neat Joe had his license plates arranged—a good sign of an efficient trucker. *Joe Wanchura*

Olson Transportation Co. of Green Bay, Wisconsin, served three states around Lake Michigan. One of the rigs that hauled those loads was this GMC and Trailmobile trailer. The power came from a Diesel engine, probably a 238 horsepower. Olson had colorful trucks with nice graphics. *Olson Transportation*

The No. 2 on the tractor meant that Seastrom Trucking of Rapid City, South Dakota, was a young and new company at this time. The two unknown drivers stood proudly beside their new White-Freightliner and new Wilson possum-belly livestock trailer when they picked up at the Wilson trailer plant in Sioux City, Iowa. *Woodworth Commercial Photos*

From Warren, Ohio, Daniels Motor Freight Inc. was a general commodities carrier that also had a steel division. The owner of this 931C Diamond T was pulling a Brown dry freight trailer on this trip. Daniels served the area from Chicago to New England and had many owner-operators in the fleet. *Neil Sherff*

Kenworth Trucks were very popular in the western states. A gentleman by the name of Randall owns this Kenworth tractor and Timpte trailer that is based in Enterprise, Utah. What you see here was a custom looking truck for this time period. *Brian Williams*

Many trucking companies, private carriers and owner-operators used Autocar trucks to pull various kinds of trailers, but Autocars were also used for towing services. This DC-75 Autocar with an integral sleeper cab was owned by the Simpsonville Garage in Simpsonville, Kentucky. A Cummins Diesel was probably the source of power. The brand name of the wrecker body is not known. *Harry Patterson*

The DCO-405 International Emeryvilles were good looking tractors. More chrome and nice paint jobs made them look even nicer. This one was a perfect example of that with the patriotic color scheme and extra chrome. The sign on the side of the Fruehauf trailer gave reference to what the cargo was on this undercover load. Ligon Specialized Haulers Inc. of Madisonville, Kentucky, was a specialized carrier of lumber, machinery, and cargo that required special handling and equipment because of size and weight. *Ligon Specialized Haulers*

Henry H. Stevens Moving and Storage Co. of Flint, Michigan, was not one of the bigger household good carriers, but they got the job done just the same. This Chevrolet, probably an AT80 series, was one of the tractors in the fleet that helped move the goods. The owner chose the optional sleeper cab. A lot of Chevrolets were used in the household goods fleets. *Neil Sherff*

In 1962, International introduced the new DC-400 series. Pictured here is a DCF-400. It had a 92-inch BBC and was available with a Cummins V6-200 or V8-265 or Detroit Diesel 6V-71 or 8V-71. They were able to pull 40-foot trailers and meet the 50-foot length limits. They were also available with sleeper cabs on longer wheelbases. *International*

The Mack B-70 series trucks were designed for the western trucker. Here we see a B-73 model that is Cummins-powered. The owner chose an add-on box sleeper instead of the factory sleeper cab. Long wheelbases, like this one, were very common in the western states. The livestock combination trailer was a Utility, but there's no identification of who the owner was. *Author's Collection*

California Marketing Co-op Inc. of Los Angeles, California, was one of many farm coops that started in the early and mid-Sixties. Most of these coops had very sharp trucks running for them because many of them were owner-operators, like Charlie Dorracker's Kenworth tractor and American reefer trailer. The colors were maroon and gold with white pin striping. *Author's Collection*

Even though Herder Truck Lines Inc. of Weimar, Texas, was not a very big company, its service was equal to that of the bigger companies. This DCO-405 International Emeryville with Trailmobile doubles was one of the teams that helped to deliver the goods to Herder's happy customers. *Herder Truck Lines Inc.*

There are two things in this picture that are popular in the West—Coors beer and the B-73 Mack. This B-73 Mack with a Fruehauf body was owned by the Yellowstone Wholesale Co. in Rock Springs, Wyoming. Every company that was contracted to haul Coors beer wore the colors of red and black. *Author's Collection*

Livestock hauling was as popular in the West as it was anywhere else in the country. One of the livestock haulers was Muldner Livestock Transport of Glendale, Arizona, and one of the rigs used was this model 352 Peterbilt with a Merritt body and trailer. Gus Muldner was the owner of the company. *Rick Manz*

Motorways of Ontario chose a 921F Diamond T to pull the Can-Car Tri-axle van trailer. The plate on the front of the trailer was most likely there so that it could be converted to a reefer trailer. *Author's Collection*

The building industry was always in need of lumber. The Arcata Redwood Company of Arcata, California, came to the rescue. This Kenworth was delivering two flatbed trailers of lumber, most likely redwood lumber. *Author's Collection*

A combination of Chevrolet and Ford trucks make up the city delivery fleet at the Illinois-California Express Inc. (I-C-X) terminal in Amarillo, Texas. The truck bodies are Browns. Notice that from left to right, number 3, 4, 5 and 6 are open-top bodies. *Mike Strueber Photography*

Kenworth trucks were very popular in California. This one was in the fleet of Cain Trucking of Tulare, California. The purpose of the unusual looking truck bodies is unknown. *Brian Williams*

C.R. England & Sons Inc. of Salt Lake City, Utah, was a cross-country produce and refrigerated carrier. One of the trucks used on the runs was this Kenworth, Tractor #26, pulling a Brown reefer trailer. The picture was taken on August 14, 1962 at the Pennsauken, New Jersey, terminal, probably after a delivery to the Philadelphia produce center. *Robert Parrish*

In 1961, Ford changed the appearance of the F-Series with different grille work and a new bumper. This Ford 800 poses nicely in front of a dirt pile to show the job that this particular truck was designed to do. This design continued up into 1969. *Ford Motor Co.*

Produce was being delivered to markets 24 hours a day, 7 days a week. This 921-F Diamond T tractor and reefer trailer are delivering some kind of produce to the James K. Wilson Produce Co. Notice the grille guard—it looks similar to the ones that are used on trucks working in the oilfields. *Author's Collection*

Moving household goods did not always require the need for a tractor-trailer. A straight truck was used when the hauling job was small enough, like this model 534 Diamond T with a sleeper cab and Matlock & Cope body. The owner was Burnham Van Service of Columbus, Georgia. *Nechtman Studio*

Kenworth trucks always opened eyes as they went down the road. Their looks and paint schemes decided that. This K-100 owned by Kraft Inc. of Brewster, Minnesota, was a good example. Little Susie and Debbie Ann were probably the driver's family. The Fruehauf cattle cruiser belonged to Thompson of Lakota, Iowa. *Neil Sherff*

Dairy and meat were the products produced by Land-O-Lakes Creameries, Inc., of Minneapolis, Minnesota. A large fleet of trucks like this DCOF-405 International Emeryville and American reefer trailer were used to deliver their products to warehouses. *Author's Collection*

This plain-jane 3-2-3-2-1 931-C Diamond T and Trailmobile dump twin was owned by Dale Osborn of Taylor, Michigan. Many axles, up to 13, were allowed in the state of Michigan. *A.T.H.S.*

Here is another Kenworth making the scene with a mixed load of freight on an oilfield-type flatbed trailer. This rig worked for the Chicago Bridge and Iron Co. of Torrance, California. Long wheelbase tractors like this one were common in the western states. *Brian Williams*

The model 931 Diamond T was a big truck that fit in with its western competitors. They were designed for and could be applied into any field of trucking. In this case, it was applied to the construction industry and was used for hauling cement blocks to the different construction sites. *Diamond T*

The most famous Mack of all times was the B Series. Many different model numbers existed in this series. Shown here is a B-67, which had the concave cab, pulling a Strick trailer. The B-67 could pull a 40-foot trailer at the 50-foot length, but because of the turning radius, for the trailer to clear the rear of the cab, the back of the cab had to be caved-in by several inches. Bringwald Transfer Inc. of Vincennes, Indiana, was the owner of the rig. *Author's Collection*

The 351 Peterbilt conventionals were popular trucks equal to the Kenworths. The first picture we have here is a model 351 that is owned by Contract Carriers, Inc. of Albuquerque, New Mexico, as it pulls a Fruehauf reefer trailer. The load is a contract load for Coors Brewing Co. in Golden, Colorado. *Neil Sherff*

The second picture is a Kenworth that is also for Contract Carriers of Albuquerque, New Mexico. It is also pulling a Fruehauf trailer hauling the same product for the same company. The colors are black and red. *Neil Sherff*

Dairy, meat, and cheese products were the commodities hauled by Midwest Coast Transport Inc. of Sioux Falls, South Dakota. Their operation in the beginning took them from the Midwest to the West Coast and in the early Sixties to the East Coast. Their fleet was made up of mostly owner-operators with various makes of trucks like this 921-F Diamond T and American reefer trailer. The tractor was sold by Frost Truck Sales in Waterloo, Iowa. *Author's Collection*

Mixer trucks were always needed in the construction business. Chickasha Transit Mix Concrete Co. in Chickasha, Oklahoma, used this model T-850 Ford to deliver the mix. It had a 477 SD V-8 engine with a 5x3 transmission on a wheelbase of 194 inches and rode on 10:00-20 tires. *Ford-Houston*

Main Lumber Co. delivered lumber in this Kenworth truck-trailer combination which was popular in the western states. An air conditioner was added to help keep the driver cool. *Brian Williams*

In the construction industry machinery needed to be transported to the job site. Taking on the job of moving the Lima shovel is an A7564T Autocar with a 170-inch wheelbase. The power came from a NH-250 Cummins Diesel with a 12-speed transmission that rode on 10:00-20 tires. The owner of the rig was Roger J. Au & Son of Mansfield, Ohio. *Autocar Trucks*

Woods Cross, Utah, was the home of the W.S. Hatch Co. They covered all the western states and hauled almost every kind of bulk material that could be hauled in trucks. They were also a big user of White-Freightliners like the one here with a Titan hopper body and pull trailer. Notice the truck was No. 215, the body was 215A and the trailer was 215B. *W.S. Hatch Co.*

Loading up for a return trip is this DCO-405 International Emeryville cab-over-engine with dual stacks and a reefer trailer. It is owned by OCOMA Foods Co. of Berryville, Arkansas. This photo could have been taken in Nogales, Arizona. *Brian Williams*

This DCO-400B International is waiting to be sold on a used truck lot. *Kenworth-Omaha*

Another reefer and produce hauler out of the South was S.W. Durrance Co. Inc. of Forest Park, Georgia. This model 931-C Diamond T tractor pulled a Great Dane reefer trailer. The picture was taken at Oriental's Truck Stop, location unknown. *Neil Sherff*

The DC-102 Autocars were always ready to take on big moving jobs. This Autocar was owned by Haddock Transportation Co., as were the Hyster "RO" series lowbed trailer and helper dolly. The load was a big Northwest crane owned by L.H. Woods & Sons of Monrovia, California. *Hyster Corp.*

Trenton, New Jersey, was the home of H.M. Royal Inc., who were manufacturers of industrial chemicals and fillers. Their products were transported in this four-hopper discharge tank trailer that is being pulled by a B-61 Mack. The rig was owned by Ro-Bo-To Trucking Inc. *Author's Collection*

Maloney Concrete Co. in Washington, D.C. owned this Ford NT-950-D. It had a V6-200 Cummins Diesel engine with a Spicer transmission. It rode on 10.00-20 tires and had a 194-inch wheelbase. *Ford-Houston*

The DCO-405 International Emeryvilles found themselves doing all kinds of hauling jobs. This one was owned by Wingert Inc. of Butler, Pennsylvania. They were contracted to pull tank-type trailers for air reduction companies, like this one hauling liquid nitrogen. Notice that the fuel tank on the tractor was rather unusual because all the Emeryvilles had the cylindrical-type fuel tanks. *Author's Collection*

Here we have another rig for Midwest Coast Transport Inc. of Sioux Falls, South Dakota, this time with a K-100 Kenworth with a reefer trailer. Midwest Coast's colors were black and green with a white band. At this time one thing that helped to decorate the tractors were the state permit numbers painted on the sides of the cab. Notice the collection of license plates and stickers that were to be part of the truck's dress code. *Neil Sherff*

This type of dump trailer was popular in the western states. The Challenge-Cook Bros. single-gate earth hauler trailer with 25-ton capacity and the 351 Peterbilt were owned by Forrest Livingston. *Author's Collection*

Here we have another famous tractor. The B-61 Mack pulled a Heil bulk tank trailer owned by Mutrie Bulk Transportation of Waltham, Massachusetts. Mutrie served the New England and Mid-Atlantic area. *Mutrie, Inc.*

Cattle hauling was a nationwide operation. Gomez Livestock Transportation Inc. of Lebanon, New Hampshire, used this White-Freightliner and Wilson possum-belly Livestock trailer to get the job done. *Neil Sherff*

Super-Valu Stores of Minneapolis, Minnesota, needed equipment that they could depend on to get the refrigerated merchandise to their store in fresh order. This model HT-950-D Ford tractor and Great Dane reefer trailer delivered wholesale groceries in Montana and the Dakotas. It was powered by a NH-250 Cummins Diesel with a Fuller R-96 transmission. The 158-inch wheelbase rode on 10.00-20 tires. *Ford-Houston*

The "P" series Diamond T was a flexible truck that could be used in almost any industry. This one was owned by Umthun Trucking Inc. of Eagle Grove, Iowa. It was fitted with a bulk feed body for farm feed delivery. The two "P" series models were the model 4300 and 5300. The 5300 model had the heavier rear end at 38,000 pounds. *Umthun Trucking*

This B-61 Mack had a long enough wheelbase to accommodate the mixer and everything needed for its operations. Wheelbases of this length for mixers were only found in the western states. *10 West Studio–Phoenix*

Most of the larger common carriers had other divisions other than their general freight. Spector Freight System Inc. of Chicago, Illinois, was one of those carriers. Here we see an owner-operator in their steel division using a model 258 Brockway to pull the spread axle steel trailer. The standard engine on the 258 was the NH-220 Cummins Diesel. It had a very short 87-inch B.B.C. The standard wheelbase was 129 inches. *Neil Sherff*

A must in any city has to be a wrecker. Johnny's Service Center on 7th and Tilghman St. in Allentown, Pennsylvania, provided 24-hour local and long-distance towing service. To do the job he used a B-61 Mack with a Holmes 750 wrecker body. Notice the gas prices at this time. *Author's Collection*

Making a trip from the Northwest down the Pacific Coast to southern California was quite a haul. However, many truckers did it, including Victor Chimicnh of Spokane, Washington. He used this K-100 Kenworth truck-trailer combination with an Aero-Liner body and Aero-Liner trailer, both equipped with reefer units. *Brian Williams*

Doing its job in the construction industry was this White 4264-Ts. The engine was a 6-200 with a MT-40 transmission and the 150-inch wheelbase rode on 10.00-20 tires. The mixer capacity was 12 cubic yards. It was owned by Canada Building Materials Ltd. of Toronto, Ontario. *White Motor Co.*

Kenworth trucks, like this model W-925, were very popular with the loggers in the Northwest. The logging trailer was a Page & Page. The rig was owned by the Weyerhauser Company in the Longview, Washington branch. Notice that the tires on the truck tandem and the trailer were of the balloon type. The model W-925 had the torsion bar suspension. *Hodge Photos*

The Texas Aluminum Co. in Rockwall, Texas, hauled aluminum and glass products in the 14 western states. To accomplish the job they decided on the model HT-950-D Ford tractor and a Hobbs 40 foot rackside trailer. The engine is a NH-220 Cummins Diesel with a Fuller R-96 10-speed Roadranger transmission. The 146-inch wheelbase rode on 10.00-22 tires. The driver got a cool ride thanks to the air conditioner. *Ford-Houston*

This cab-style GMC was nicknamed the "cracker box." They weren't the prettiest looking cabs but many companies used them. This GMC owner decided to fancy his up with extra chrome and his own paint design. It all added up to a pretty sharp looking GMC as it went down the road pulling for Western Trucking Co. of St. Louis, Missouri. The power was likely from a 238 Detroit Diesel. *Author's Collection*

A good impression of any business is neatness and appearance. With a lot of extra chrome items and nice paint job, this B-61 Mack for Slick Auto Parts of Inwood, Long Island, New York, made them feel proud of the job they do. *Harry Patterson*

Canadians also liked Autocar trucks. This DC-7564T was owned by Irving Oil Company Ltd. of St. Johns, New Brunswick, Canada. The engine was 250 horsepower with a 10-speed transmission and ran on 11:00-20 tires. The customer decided that they wanted the steel construction-type fenders. *Autocar Trucks*

In 1963, White-Freightliner designed a whole new breed of truck. It was the half-cab WFHD-62, available as a 6x4, 6x6 or 8x4. The wheelbases ranged from 175 to 235 inches. The standard engine was a C-180 Cummins Diesel with a Fuller 5-speed transmission. Other options were available. The half cab was able to be used in several applications like a dump, block hauler, or bulk feed tanker. Here we see it with a mixer body. Reid Sand & Gravel chose the optional floatation tires. *Author's Collection*

Abner A. Wolf Inc. delivered refrigerated products for freshness. The job was done by the help of this model C-1000 Ford and Fruehauf reefer trailer. The source of power was a 477 V-4 engine with a MT-42 transmatic transmission. The wheelbase was 111 inches and rode on 10.00-20 tires. The company was from Detroit, Michigan. *Ford-Houston*

When we see double 40-foot trailers, we think of the Indiana, Ohio, Massachusetts pike and the New York state thruway. But, there was also the Kansas turnpike where this set of 40s was operating. A White 5000 was pulling the set, a Trailmobile open-top and a Fruehauf reefer. Consolidated Freightways inc. of Menlo Park, California, was the company that was operating them. *Kansas Turnpike*

Whether it was to the races or to a show, the horses had to be transported in order to participate. Ralph G. Smith Inc. of West Chester, Pennsylvania, did the job with this Brokway tractor and Dorsey horse van. Notice the lucky horseshoe. *Harry Patterson*

This DC-9564-T had a 290-horsepower supercharged Diesel engine with a 15-speed transmission. The wheelbase was 142.5 inches with 11.00-22 tires on the front and 10.00-20 tires on the rear. This rig was owned by Main Sand and Gravel in Detroit, Michigan. The 2-2-3-2-1 is the Michigan Special. *Autocar Trucks*

Another dump rig here, although not as long, was this F-1000-D Ford for the Reading Anthracite Coal Co. of Pottsville, Pennsylvania. The engine was a V6-200 Cummins Diesel with a Spicer transmission. The wheelbase was 146 inches and rode on 10.00-22 tires. They claim it averaged 6.6 mpg with 62,000-pounds gross while hauling coal. *Ford-Houston*

This DCO-405 International Emeryville was taking a rest while being loaded or unloaded. Hawaiian Punch was likely the cargo in this Trailmobile reefer trailer. The company chose the bigger 80-inch sleeper cab for the driver and added dual stacks. *Neil Sherff*

Standing beside his truck, this 1963 Kenworth was owned by D. Schuoler of Yakima, Washington. Not much information is known, but there are two things to note. The first is to notice the position of the stack coming up behind the sleeper. This was very rare on Kenworth trucks. Second, is that this photo was taken in 1973 and at this time this truck had seen its second millionth mile. It sure looks great for 10 years old. *Kenworth Truck Co.*

Another Ford doing construction work was this T-850 owned by W.J. Jones Trucking Co. of Hales Corners, Wisconsin. The engine was a 477 SD V-8 with a MT-42 transmatic transmission. The wheelbase was 176 inches with an 11,000-pound front axle and a 34,000-pound rear axle that rode on 10.00-20 tires. The unit grossed 44,000 pounds. *Ford-Houston*

Mack's workhorse of the West was the model B-73. The owner had it leased on with W.J. Digby Co. in Denver, Colorado, a hauler of refrigerated products throughout the western states. *Author's Collection*

The Brockway model 260 was a popular truck in the mid-Atlantic and New England area. This tractor, the 260 L, was powered by Brockway's model 48 BD six-cylinder engine. The Amherst Oil Co. in Amherst, Massachusetts, used this one to pull one of their tanker trailers. *Brockway Trucks*

L.R. Denny Inc. was a bulk hauler based in California. This set of bottom hopper tank trailers were being pulled by a model 288 Peterbilt that was powered by a Caterpillar Diesel engine. Here it was being loaded at the plant of Livingston, Graham Inc. *Caterpillar Co.*

Many manufacturing companies had their own private fleets of trucks. One of those companies was Georgia-Pacific Corp. based in Tigard, Oregon. They had a fleet of trucks to begin the operation of hauling logs from forest to plant and a fleet of trucks to haul the finished product from plant to customer. Here we see a White-Freightliner with a Utility dromedary body pulling a Utility trailer. The lucky driver of this rig got four air horns, air conditioner, chrome stack, and extra road lights, which is rather unusual for a company rig. *Neil Sherff*

This is the side view of the tractor showing the dromedary body which looks like it's loaded with rolls of paper. Notice the no-hole wheels on the font wheels. *Neil Sherff*

Here we have two brothers and one step-brother. The two brothers are the B-61 and the B-73 Macks. The step-brother is the C-600 Mack. Notice the hood on the B-73 is longer than the hood on the B-61, and the hood on the C-600 is a lot shorter. Also notice that the cab on the C-600 sits a lot higher than the other two cabs. Brown introduced a new tank trailer, here being pulled by the C-600. The tank trailer on the far right is a Great Dane. *Author's Collection*

Another tanker group are these Michigan-type tankers. The tractors are K-100 Kenworths with 52-inch cabs. The tank trailers are Fruehauf. *Author's Collection*

Big 3 Industrial Gases in West Palm Beach, Florida, had this White-Freightliner and Delta tank trailer in the their fleet. For defense against the hot Florida sunshine, the driver had an air-conditioned cab. *Author's Collection*

When the owner of this GMC purchased it new in 1964, he probably never thought that he would be driving this tractor some 41 years later, finally retiring it in 2005. The rig was leased to Kirk Trucking Service in Delmont, Pennsylvania. Once the rig was paid off, everything after that was money in the bank. *John Hiestand*

One of the larger carriers was Wilson Freight Co. of Cincinnati, Ohio. They covered the area form Kansas to New England. Most of their tractors were Macks, Whites, GMCs, and a few Fords. This "N" series Ford did duty pulling a Gindy trailer. This could have been a tractor in the city delivery fleet. *Wilson Freight Co.*

From the land of the lone-star state we have E.T.M.F.-East Texas Motor Freight Inc. of Dallas, Texas. They covered an area up through the middle of the country from the Great Lakes to the Gulf. Their fleet at this time consisted of the newly restyled model 9000 Whites with some Lufkin trailers. *East Texas Motor Freight*

One of the two biggest companies over the years was Roadway Express Inc. of Akron, Ohio. Roadway had a fleet of tractors that consisted mainly of Macks, Whites, Fords Internationals and GMCs. However, some Dodge tractors made their way into the fleet like this 900 series that pulled a Stick trailer. One thing to mention is that almost all Roadway tractors had trailer-high stacks. *Roadway Express, Inc.*

International offered a host of various wheelbase lengths and a few different cab sizes. This DCOF-405 Emeryville, owned by Baker Commodities Inc., had the 52-inch cab but the wheelbase was unknown. *Trig Svendsen Photography*

When it was time to go to bed, the bedroom was on the third floor. Entrance to the third-floor bedroom was made by crawling up through the top of the cab. White Freightliner designed this 48-inch cab to gain more cargo space for livestock. A lot of livestock haulers used these truck-trailer combinations. Livestock Transport Co. was the owner of this one. *Brian Williams*

One of the big monstrous trucks in the West was the DC-10064F Autocar. Long wheelbases were typical of many conventional tractors that ran west. Fruit and produce were being hauled in the reefer trailer that belonged to Russell Miller Fruit & Produce Co. *Author's Collection*

The driver of this "D" series GMC added a little bit of fancy to his truck with dual air horns, pin striping and extra lights. Not only that, but he also added a big 8V-71 Detroit Diesel for more power. The truck was owned by B&M Smith Produce of Honeoye Falls, New York, and here pulled an early Fifties Fruehauf produce trailer. *Neil Sherff*

Here we have another "D" series GMC with a day cab. It was owned by Curis Keal Transport co. Inc. of Cleveland, Ohio. Here it hauled a Euclid dump truck on the lowbed Fruehauf trailer. Notice that the outriggers had to be used because of the width of the load. *Harold Ekers Photo*

Boats sail on water but to get them to water they must sail across our American highways by truck. Whittaker Marine and Mfg. Co. in Winona, Minnesota, manufactured Whit-Craft House Boats and transported this one on a Kenworth K-121 with a LaCross lowbed trailer. The truck was sold through Rihm Motor Co. in St. Paul, Minnesota. *Dufrey Studios*

Mack Trucks donated this F-600 tractor to pull the Trailmobile trailer for *Pace Magazine*. The F series was introduced in 1962 and went way into the Seventies. Three cab sizes were available at 50, 72 or 80 inches. It had a large two-piece windshield which made for good viewing. The new 711 thermodyne engine was offered in the F series. *Author's Collection*

One of the largest tankers and bulk haulers in the nation was E. Brooke Matlack Inc. in Lansdown, Pennsylvania. They had a variety of different makes of tractors and various types of tank trailers. The tractor here was a model-9000 White that pulled a tank trailer hauling raw fluid. *Robert Parrish*

The owner-operators who had the Canadian-made Hayes tractors liked to fancy them up a little like the American owner-operators. This long wheelbase tractor with a rackside dromedary body sported dual chrome stacks. This Hayes Clipper cab-over-engine worked for K&M Transport Ltd. of Calgary, Alberta. *Author's Collection*

Mayflower Transit Co. Inc. of Indianapolis, Indiana, was probably the country's largest moving company. The fleet was made up of many owner-operators with all different makes of tractors. Here we see a colorful GMC with a matching Trailmobile moving van trailer. Mayflower had many agents across the country that owned their own equipment. *Mayflower Transit*

Livestock hauling was done in either tractor-trailer or truck-trailer combinations, or double trailers like we see here. This White-Freightliner tractor that was owned by Warren Williams of N. Portland, Oregon, pulled this set of Merritt possum-belly trailers. Just for your information there were 1,600 vent holes in each trailer. *Author's Collection*

At this time, the model 351 Peterbilt was becoming a popular conventional tractor with the owner-operators. The Chocktaw Distributing Company in Broken Bow, Oklahoma, had this one pulling a Hobbs trailer in their fleet. In this time period this was considered a customized truck. By today's standards it is considered a standard tractor. Hobbs trailers were very popular in the Southeast. *Brian Williams*

The A-100 Autocars were a popular western-style truck because of their ruggedness and being all-aluminum which made them lighter and able to haul more weight. The propane tank body and trailer made a great looking truck-trailer combination on this Autocar. *Author's Collection*

This fancied up F-700 Mack sported dual chrome stacks, dual air horns, chrome bumper, and an air conditioner. This F-700 (the tractor number was R-700) was in the fleet of Rice Truck Lines of Great Falls, Montana. The gasoline truck body and trailer were made by Beall. *Author's Collection*

Shupe Bros. in Greeley, Colorado, hauled a lot of grain and feed for the Monfort feed lots of the Monfort Packing Co. in Greeley, Colorado. They also hauled salt. The grain and feed were hauled in Timpte grain trailers that were pulled by W-900 Kenworths. Their area covered some of the western and midwestern states. *Neil Sherff*

Here we have a livestock rig that is of the tractor-trailer type. The tractor is a White-Freightliner that is pulling a Hobbs drop floor livestock trailer. The owner of the truck is Noble Danner of Oklahoma City, Oklahoma. The gentlemen standing beside the rig could be none other than Noble Danner himself. Glancing at the state permits on the cab, it looks like this rig covered a lot of territory. *Geo. T. Hale Photography*

The DCF-400 International was a popular tractor with Indianhead Truck Lines Inc. of St. Paul, Minnesota. They had a lot of Internationals in their fleet, this one pulling a Brown trailer. Their huge windshield made for good visibility. The D-400 series was the replacement for the previous RD-300 and RD-400. *Indianhead Truck Lines*

Alan Kramer got this AW10264 Autocar with a NH-250-horsepower Diesel and a 5x4 transmission for his log hauling venture. It rode on 10:00-22 tires stretched out on a 240-inch wheelbase. The truck was leased on with Kramer & Smith Logging of Coos Bay, Oregon. *Autocar Trucks/A.T.H.S.*

This nice and neatly stacked load of lumber was headed for who knows where. The lumber was from the Kiabab Lumber Co. who was also the deliverer. The move was done by using a K-100 Kenworth and a Fruehauf flatbed trailer. Ten bunches made up the load. *Author's collection*

Provost Cartage Inc. of Montreal, Quebec, had a large fleet of trucks and trailers. They operated as a common carrier and all bulk commodities hauler. They had dump, flatbed, and many different types of tank trailers. This B-73 Mack was converted to a tandem axle tractor by using a Jo-Dog. The tri-axle tank trailer was used for hauling acid. *Provost Cartage*

Here is a White-Freightliner with a Merritt body and Merritt pull trailer for hauling livestock. Zwang is the only visible name on the door. It is a California-based truck. Notice the huge fuel tank. *Author's Collection*

Another cattle rig was this K-100 Kenworth and Wilson possum-belly livestock trailer. It was owned by Robert Kidd Inc. of Neponset, Illinois. Kenworth trucks were becoming more popular with the livestock haulers. The Chicago stockyard was a busy place. *Neil Sherff*

It looks like the driver was taking care of some paperwork while waiting to get a load. This K-100 Kenworth with a Merritt body and possum-belly trailer was either owned by or leased to Muldner Livestock Transportation of Glendale, Arizona. *Author's Collection*

The Cosmodyne Corp. manufactured regular and special types of tank trailers. The Cosmodyne Goody and pull trailer were made for the Chevron Corp. to haul gasoline. The body was mounted on a White-Freightliner truck. *Author's Collection*

Some trailers are not very ordinary. This example here shows two bottom hopper bulk hauling trailers. It's unknown what kind of bulk commodities were being hauled in them. The model 282 Peterbilt pulling the set was owned by Prouty Trucking of Turlock, California. *Brian Williams*

Glibert Carrier Corp. of New York City, New York, hauled a lot of garment out of New York City's garment district. At this time, Gilbert used all DCO-405 International Emeryvilles, most of them with dromedary bodies. Later on they had some Kenworths and White-Freightliners. The picture was taken on April 18, 1965 off the Ohio turnpike. *Neil Sherff*

The DCV-7264 was introduced around 1962. It was different from the other Autocar models because of the much higher 1400D which in turn made the cab sit higher. It had a high Aero-Liner sleeper box and pulled a Trailmobile reefer trailer. The rig was leased on with Great Markwestern Packing Co. of Detroit, Michigan. The picture was taken in 1968 coming out of the toll booth of the Pennsylvania turnpike at the Carlisle exit. *Ron Adams*

This model 990 Diamond T was in the fleet of Campbells "66" Express Inc. of Springfield, Missouri. The picture boasts of the company's 38-year history—9,200 miles of certified routes servicing 600 communities in nine states, with 2,000 employees and a "a few old grouches!" The camel on the Fruehauf trailer shows that they are "humpin to please." This was the company slogan for a long time. *Campbells "66" Express*

The 400 series Brockway used the Mack F model cab and was available with a 50-, 72-, or 80-inch cab, B.B.C. Cummins and Detroit Diesels were available along with a gasoline 48 BD 6 in-line engine and also a variety of transmissions. *Brockway Trucks*

This model 281 Peterbilt and its set of double rackside trailers were taking a break from a long, hard upgrade pull. By the decal on the door it seemed that the main commodities hauled were fruits and berries. Notice that by now three bars were added across the grille. *Brian Williams*

The owner of this DCO-405 International Emeryville thought he would give the front a little different appearance. To change the appearance he used the grille work from the Diamond Reo "Royale." The Emeryville pulled this Great Dane reefer trailer for Lee Produce of Sanford, Florida. *Author's Collection*

Greenstein Trucking Co. was a big reefer and produce hauler out of Pompano Beach, Florida. The fleet of leased tractors was made up of all different makes. One of those makes was this F-700 Mack with a Fruehauf reefer trailer. Greenstein covered the eastern half of the United States. *Neil Sherff*

The F-model became very well liked by the companies and owner-operators. This FL-700 Mack Western was leased on with Trans-Cold Express Inc. of Dallas, Texas. Trans-Cold Express Inc. was a nationwide reefer hauler that hauled a lot of swinging beef out of Texas to the New England area. They were one of the companies that were owned by Midwest-Emery Freight System of Chicago, Illinois. The picture was taken in 1968 at the Roadway Truck Stop at Carlisle, Pennsylvania. *Ron Adams*

At the Roadway truck stop was this Diamond T 1064FL known as the Westerner. Various engines were offered along with various types of transmissions. This owner-operator leased his truck to TransAmerican Freight Lines Inc. of Detroit, Michigan. It pulled a Fruehauf reefer trailer. *Robert Parrish*

This moving van for Mayflower Transit Co. of Indianapolis, Indiana, was on its way to deliver the household belongings to someone relocating. This Ford C-700 with Kentucky moving van trailer was owned by R.E. Hill. *Robert Young Studio*

This White-Freightliner was taking delivery of a set of Merritt bottom hopper grain trailers. Merritt was a builder and manufacturer of truck bodies and trailers used for hauling livestock and agricultural commodities. *Merritt Equipment Co.*

The 260 Brockway was a sturdy-built truck. The standard engine was the NH-220 Cummins Diesel. Commercial Transportation Co. of Gainesville, Georgia, had this one to pull a Brown reefer trailer. Take notice of the high breather, the standing platform on top of the sleeper—the sleeper and cab are one piece. The picture was taken on June 8, 1966 at the Toledo 5 truck stop. *Neil Sherff*

Part of the fleet of C-600 Macks are backed up to the dock at the Camden, New Jersey, terminal for Nelson Freightways Inc. of Rockville, Connecticut. The C model was made from 1963 to 1965. A total of 1,589 were produced. The picture was taken on May 30, 1965 in Camden, New Jersey. *Robert Parrish*

The only coast-to-coast carrier since 1946 was Denver-Chicago Trucking Co. Inc. of Denver, Colorado. However, that changed in 1960. This K-100 Kenworth and reefer trailer stopped for a break at the turnpike station at North Lima, Ohio. The 800 series numbers were based in Chicago and Detroit to run east. Denver-Chicago Trucking Co. Inc. was one of the popular common carriers. The picture was taken on April 4, 1965. *Robert Parrish*

For many years, North American Van Lines had the same color scheme. In the mid-Sixties they decided it was time to take on a new look. The colors of red, cream and white were selected like on this Kentucky moving van trailer and red and white for the tractors as displayed on this DCO-405 International Emeryville with the 80-inch cab. Their home office was in Fort Wayne, Indiana. *Oscar & Associates*

Leonard Bros. Transfer Co. of Miami, Florida, was a heavy hauler of government loads, heavy equipment, and cumbersome freight. Here we see two 100-foot long steel girders weighing in at 27 tons each, going to the 22 Avenue Bridge for the Nashville Bridge Co. on July 16, 1965. To move the two bridge girders, Leonard Bros. decided to use a B61 Mack. *Leonard Bros. Transfer*

Lowbed trailers were built strong to handle those big heavy loads like this big D8 Caterpillar. The tractor was a K-100 Kenworth owned by Dean Hanes Machinery Co. and was powered by a Caterpillar Diesel engine. *Bailey Studio*

Tri-State Motor Transit Co. Inc. of Joplin, Missouri, was a hauler of machinery, ammunition, aircraft equipment and government loads. One of the rigs in the fleet was this White-Freightliner and Fruehauf trailer. Although this was a company rig, they did have some owner-operators pulling for them. Notice the line-up of state permit numbers on the cab. *Tri-State Motor Transit*

North American Van Lines Inc. was based in Fort Wayne, Indiana. The White 2000 sleeper was pulling a single-axle moving van trailer. *Harry Patterson*

Big dromedary bodies were used in the western states to use up the empty space on long wheelbase tractors where longer length limits were allowed for light freight. American Can Co. took advantage of the dromedary body and mounted it on a White-Freightliner tractor with a Utility body and trailer. *Author's Collection*

Brada-Miller Freight System Inc. in Kokomo, Indiana, was a big hauler of steel and steel products. The fleet was made up of owner-operators like this White-Freightliner pulling a tri-axle flatbed trailer. Plenty of chrome and Michigan-style pin striping made Brada-Miller proud to have a rig like this one leased in their fleet. *Neil Sherff*

Here is another rig wearing the Coors graphics near Nogales, Arizona. The W-900 Kenworth and Brown reefer trailer make a nice pair. The owner of the rig is unknown but he surely can feel proud of its appearance. *Brian Williams*

Around the mid-Sixties, Wilson started to change the design on the front and sides of its livestock trailers. This model 352 Peterbilt and the new trailer for Armstrong in Austin, Minnesota, was backed up to the loading shoot to take on its first load. *Woodworth Photos, Wilson Trailer Co.*

The model 258 Brockway had a short 87-inch BBC. With a sleeper it was 112 inches BBC. The engine was a NH-220 Cummins Diesel, housed with swing-out fenders for easy access to the engine. This model 258 had the add-on box sleeper and dual stacks hauling a load of steel pipes on this flatbed trailer for Youngstown Cartage Co. of Youngstown, Ohio. The picture was taken in 1968 at Hirshmans truck stop. *Ron Adams*

This cab doesn't look much like a Diamond T, but it is. It is a 931C with the upper grille bars removed and the four lower chrome bars from the cab-over-engine model of the Fifties. This fancied up Diamond T is pulling a rackside trailer for Spector Freight System in their steel division. *Harry Patterson*

1966 was the year that Mack introduced the new DM series which was a dump and mixer. All DM models had the offset cab which was the same cab used on the U model. The gross vehicle weight on this DM-600 SX was 66,000 to 76,000 pounds. This one came with a Challenge mixer body. *Mack Trucks*

This DF-405 International was made to be a logging truck. It was also the 1966 logger show truck. It had a 114-inch BBC and was powered by a NH Cummins Diesel. Optional Diesel engines were offered along with a variety of transmissions. *International*

With new graphics and color scheme, this White 3000 sleeper cab with a Fruehauf moving van trailer hauled for North American Van Lines Inc. of Fort Wayne, Indiana. These model 3000 Whites were plentiful in the moving industry. *Harry Patterson*

Equipped with a flat bed body for hauling blocks, this WFHD 6264 White-Freightliner carried its load on a 175-inch wheelbase. The standard engine was a C-180 Cummins. Smithwick Concrete Products was the owner of this block hauler. *White-Freightliner*

These low cab-over-engine Chevrolets were popular with household goods carriers. Single-axle moving van trailers, like this Trailmobile, were what the moving industry used until about the early to mid-Sixties when they started to use tandem axle trailers. Take notice of the sleeper box behind the cab. *Robert Parrish*

The Azar Nut Company was in El Paso, Texas. The picture was also taken in El Paso, Texas. This 352 Peterbilt and Utility trailer were owned by Terminal Truck Leasing Inc. The chrome helped to show off the Peterbilt paint design. At this time this was considered a customized truck. *Harry Patterson*

This was the last style for Diamond T with their cab-over-engine line before it became Diamond Reo in 1967. This one was with National Truck Service and pulled a Hobbs Vangard reefer trailer hauling produce. The driver enjoyed the comforts of an air conditioner. *Brian Williams*

A 50-inch day cab was selected to do local area hauling on this International CO-4000 that pulled a Certified tank trailer. The CO-4000 was introduced in 1965 to replace the DCO-405 Emeryville. *Commercial Photography*

The A75 Autocar was an aluminum-built tractor that many owner-operators liked because it made for a lighter tractor that hauled more payload. One of those A75s was this one leased to Trans-Cold Express Inc. of Dallas, Texas. Trans-Cold Express Inc. hauled a lot of Texas Swinging Beef in this Utility reefer trailer to the Midwest and the northeastern states. *Harry Patterson*

This 1000 series Dodge also had its place in the trucking field. It was powered by a Cummins Diesel and used a Brown produce trailer to do this particular job. There was a big sleeper box for the driver to rest in. *Author's Collection*

In 1966, Strickland Transportation Co. of Dallas, Texas, took delivery of a fleet of new model 7000 Whites. Day cabs were selected with air conditioners. Strickland covered from Texas up through the Midwest to Chicago and the Great Lakes and then on to the East Coast. Strickland tractors always had trailer high stacks. *Strickland Trans. Co.*

Cattle hauling was very popular in and around the state of Iowa. M. Wilken and Son of Westside, Iowa, went to Hampton to pick up their new Jason-Chamberlin livestock trailer. They used a model 352 Peterbilt to tote it home. Could the duo be M. Wilden and his son? *Jason-Chamberlin Co.*

DC International became the new name for Denver-Chicago Trucking Co. in the mid-Sixties. The DC fleet at this time was almost all K-100 Kenworths. Number 292 was assigned to the Denver-Chicago run. It was pulling a brand new 40-foot Strick trailer. *DC International*

The new CO-4000 was becoming equally as popular as its predecessor, the DCO-405 Emeryville. Trucking companies and owner-operators took to them. Cyrus Truck Lines Inc. of Iola, Kansas, used this one to pull one of their gasoline tank trailers. *Shaw Studios*

This plain-jane A-7564 Autocar with a day cab looked nice coupled up to the red Jason-Chamberlin 35-foot grain trailer. The rig was owned by Obermeyer Grain Co. in Kokomo, Indiana. *Jason-Chamberlin Co.*

Decked out with plenty of chrome and a great looking color scheme, this 1966 model 352 Peterbilt with a Brown flatbed trailer was owned by C&T Trucking Co. of Oakland, California. *C&T Trucking Co.*

Whatever kind of produce that was on this load, it got shipped in style. Notice how the polished aluminum wheels shine on 351 Peterbilt and the Brown reefer trailer. Bert-O-Lino Produce Co. in San Diego, California, was the hauler. The driver rested comfortably in the 48-inch box sleeper and kept cool at the same time thanks to the air conditioner. *Brian Williams*

This rig was owned by the Freeman Chemical Corp. of New Washington, Wisconsin. The White-Freightliner pulled the Kari-Kool 8,600-gallon 3-compartment chemical tank trailer. *Author's Collection*

The R series Mack turned out to be as popular as the previous B series. This RL-700 and Hyde drop floor livestock trailer was owned by Emmett Montgomery of Stevensville, Texas. The dual stacks suggest that it could have been powered by a 318 8V-71 Detroit Diesel. *Harry Patterson*

Bob Workman was a truck driver who took pride in the equipment that he owned and drove. His 1966 W-900 Kenworth with matching Fruehauf trailer did not fall short on chrome. He leased this rig to All States Freight Inc. of Akron, Ohio. The year 1966 was the last for All States as P.I.E. took over their operations. *Neil Sherff*

For produce haulers, the Philadelphia Produce Center was the place to be. Trucks came there from all around the country. Raymond Bolzan Inc., produce grower from Great Meadows, New Jersey, hauled his produce there with this Ford 800 series and TBC produce body. The picture was taken on July 17, 1966. *Robert Parrish*

Canadian Freightways Ltd. of Calgary, Alberta, Canada, was the Canadian Division of American Consolidated Freightways Inc. based in Menlo Park, California. The White-Freightliner had a long enough wheelbase to accommodate the Aero-Liner dromedary body and also pull an Aero-Liner reefer trailer. Western Canada ran the same types of equipment used in the western United States. *Canadian Freightways*

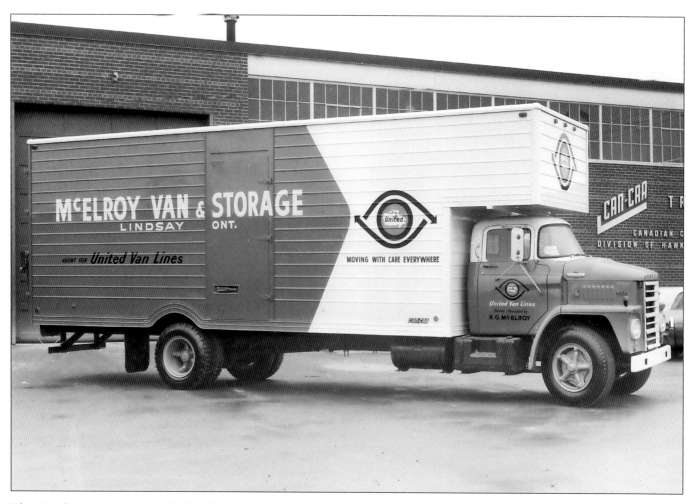

This Dodge 500 series worked well for McElry Van & Storage of Lindsay, Ontario, Canada, one of the Canadian agents for United Van Lines. Notice the Can-Car body extension over the cab. Some bodies had the extension overhang all the way to the front of the hood. *Micklethwaite Photo*

North American Van Lines Inc. of Ft. Wayne, Indiana, showed off the new graphics for the company around 1966. They are displayed on the GMC tractor and Kentucky moving van trailer. Nicknamed "cracker box" GMCs, trucks like this were used by a lot of for-hire common carriers and owner-operators. *Neil Sherff*

One of the biggest for-hire common carriers on the Eastern Seaboard was Johnson Motor Lines Inc. of Charlotte, North Carolina. They had a variety of equipment to serve the customer's needs, like this Strick Converta flat trailer and DCO-405 International Emeryville. Johnson was always a big International customer. Johnson served the area from the Gulf Coast up along the Atlantic Coast on up into the New England states. *Robert Parrish*

Peters Bros. Livestock Hauling, based in Lenhartsville, Pennsylvania, hauled livestock from the Chicago stockyards and throughout the Midwest into Allentown, Pennsylvania, and other northeastern points. At this time their fleet consisted mostly of Kenworth K-100 cab-over-engines with this one being their first W-900. It pulled a Wilson livestock trailer, nicknamed the "Cabbage Cutter." Peters Bros. were in the livestock hauling business in 1952 and switched from livestock to reefer hauling in the late 1980s. *Peters Bros. Inc.*

The Amway Xcorp. had a fleet of trucks that were leased, like this Diamond T tractor and spread-axle three-bay bulk tank trailer. The appearance of the mid-Sixties Diamond T was a little different than the early Sixties because of the seven chrome bars. *Author's Collection*

The Ralston Purina Co. was a nationwide producer of feed for poultry and livestock. They had their own fleet of trucks, easy to spot with the checkerboard square signs. This White 9000 was based at the company's plant in Pocatello, Idaho. *Ralston Purina Co.*

Long wheelbase tractors always looked good, like this White-Freightliner with a Fruehauf reefer trailer. The owner was Wayne Gibson of Portland, Oregon. All the chrome and the extras made this rig one nice piece of equipment. *A.T.H.S.*

The "U" model Mack was a strange looking tractor because of the offset cab. The advantage to this was that the driver had a better view of what was in front of him with the cab moved 11 inches to the left. *Mack Trucks Inc.*

The Standard Oil Co., a division of the American Oil Co., had a nationwide fleet of trucks. This one was a White-Freightliner truck with a Beall body and pull trailer. These truck-trailer rigs were a common sight. *Beall Trailers*

This Canadian Kenworth model L-924 was either being loaded or unloading onto the rail car. Notice the rack over the cab for protection. *Author's Collection*

The Halliburton Company of Duncan, Oklahoma, had many Internationals in their fleet. Halliburton used an International Fleetstar to haul this confusing group of machinery that was probably used for cementing up oil wells. *Halliburton*

Every now and then there was an unusual-looking truck engineered by the owner to suit his or her own taste, like this high-rise Chevy. What this owner did here was the same thing that Ford did with their H-1000 series by using the C model Ford cab. The rig was leased on with Federal Warehouse Co. who were agents for Allied Van Lines of Broadview, Illinois. *Harry Patterson*

When P.I.E. became a coast-to-coast carrier in 1966 with the purchase of All States Freight Inc., all of the All States equipment was replaced. Some of the replacements were these lightweight aluminum Mack FL-700s. The Fruhauf trailers were also a popular trailer with P.I.E. *Robert Parrish*

Wamix Ready Mixed Concrete of Dallas, Texas, decided to choose an Autocar to work for them. Spread out on a 174-inch wheelbase, this model DC-9364 was powered by a 190-horsepower Diesel engine teamed up with a 20-speed transmission. It had a 50,000-pound rear axle and an 8-cubic-yard mixer with everything riding on 11.00-22 tires. *Autocar Trucks*

Disabled vehicles appreciated a truck like this. The G&M Auto Co. in Cleveland, Ohio, used this model 4000 White for towing purposes. Noticc the 2-way radio that was used to keep in contact with home base. *Scope Foto Arts*

The "F" series Mack Western was popular with many owner-operators. This FL-700 joined the special commodities reefer division of Navajo Freight Lines Inc. of Denver, Colorado, as it ran coast-to-coast. The commodities rode in a Utility reefer trailer. The picture was taken at Tooley's truck terminal in New Jersey. *Harry Patterson*

California-based Sandberg Furniture used a model 282 Peterbilt and this set of Utility trailers to haul their products. Notice the side window in the 73-inch cab and how the fuel tank and sander was squeezed between the front and rear axles. *Author's Collection*

The 400 series Brockway came in three models—456, 457 and 459—with either the 50-inch day cab or the 80-inch sleeper cab. Here, the 80-inch sleeper was pulling a Great Dane reefer trailer. *Harry Patterson*

This DCF-400 showed off its ability to handle the Superior dump body and trailer. This series ran into 1972 and had equally as many uses as its predecessors, the RD-300 and RD-400 series. *Keystone Photography*

This RL-700 Mack Western was all lightweight aluminum. It was owned by the Shell Oil Co. and used for hauling gasoline. *Author's Collection*

This GMC 7500 series was doing its duty for Williams Moving and Storage Co. in Cranbrook, British Columbia. Its partner was this Freuhauf moving van trailer. There were no fancy extras on this truck but it was still a nice and clean looking truck. *Author's Collection*

The Airport Machinery Corp. of Austin, Texas, employed this model 7000 White to pull one of their rackside trailers. The driver had the comfort of an air conditioner. The dual stacks on this tractor were rather unusual for this model. *Harry Patterson*

This CO-4000 International that was owned by C-H-B Fine Foods of Pico Rivera, California, had a 50-inch air-conditioned cab. It pulled a set of Pike trailers. C-H-B was founded in 1859 and had a variety of food products. *Brian Williams*

Owned by Texaco, this rear shot of a set of Michigan-type doubles had a 2-2-3-2-1 set-up. The Fruehauf double tankers were being pulled by an "F" model Mack. Imagine what it looked like from the front. *Author's Collection*

Livestock hauling was plentiful in the mid-section of the country, naturally because this was the agricultural area. George Sears of Atkinson, Illinois, was one of the haulers from that area. He used a C60 Chevrolet tractor and a Transport livestock trailer. *Transport Trailers Inc.*

Denver-Chicago Trucking Co. Inc. of Denver, Colorado, mostly had the western-style trucks of Kenworths, White-Freightliners and Internationals in their fleet at this time. However, there were a few strays among the group like this 800 series Dodge. It was most likely used for the P.U.D. city fleet for the heavier jobs. The trailer is a Converta flat. *Denver-Chicago Trucking Co.*

Another Denver-Chicago Trucking Co. rig was this Loadstar 1700 International. This one was pulling a rackside trailer that may have been on its way to be teamed up as a set of doubles. *Denver-Chicago Trucking Co.*

The site where this picture was taken was at the old Flemmings truck stop just at the entrance ramp to the turnpike at Carlisle, in 1968. The "R" model Mack with a flatbed trailer worked for C&H Transportation Co. Inc. of Dallas, Texas. *Ron Adams*

The model 352 Peterbilt was becoming a very popular cab-over-engine tractor with the owner-operators in the eastern states during this time period. This truck, photographed in May of 1967, was either a 352 stock tractor or one ordered by a customer through the Keystone Peterbilt dealer in Lancaster, Pennsylvania. *Barton Henley*

The 9500 GMC came in two versions, the short hood and long hood. This short hood version rig was owned by T.A. Graham of Dayton, Ohio, and pulled a Trailmobile reefer trailer. The tractor was powered by a Cummins Diesel engine. *Author's Collection*

This DC6366 Autocar Diesel was a six-wheeler with six-wheel drive. *Autocar Trucks*

This DC-6766 Autocar Diesel was also a six-wheeler with six-wheel drive. The GVW on this truck was 56,000 pounds. *Autocar Trucks*

This model 352 Peterbilt with a long wheelbase, a dromedary body and Utility trailer made use of all the available space when hauling lightweight freight to gain all the volume possible. Notice where the fifth wheel was positioned in order to hook up the trailer. *Author's Collection*

This CO-4000 International was taking a break so it could cool down the engine after a long hard pull up the grade. A 50-inch cab was ordered along with a flatbed dromedary body and here pulled a flatbed trailer. The load is some kind of sheet metal manufactured by the Griffin Steel and Supply Co. *Brian Williams*

This is a truck that lived two lives. The first life was as a tractor for pulling trailers and its second life was as a winch truck for unloading cargo off flatbed trailers as seen here. This DC-10264, owned by the Platte Pipe Line Company in Casper, Wyoming, had a 260-inch wheelbase powered by a NH-220 Cummins Diesel engine with a 5x4 transmission. It rode on 11.00-20 tires and easily hauled this 15,000-pound electric motor. *Autocar Trucks/A.T.H.S.*

Utility companies used Autocar Trucks, like this model 3700U with a 186-horsepower gasoline engine and MT-40 6-speed automatic transmission. It rode on 9.00-20 tires and had a 120-inch wheelbase. This four-man crew cab was owned by Iroquois Gas Corp. of Buffalo, New York. *Autocar Trucks*

The owner of this CO-4000 International gave it his own paint scheme and some extra chrome to suit his taste. Hartline of Valley Head, Alabama, owned the rig. Here it pulled a Hobbs Vanguard reefer trailer, the whole set-up proudly photographed at the Jersey Truck Center in Jersey City, New Jersey. *Harry Patterson*

Unit Parts Co. in Oklahoma City, Oklahoma, decided to rent from Ryder Truck Rentals instead of buying a truck. This CO-4000 had an air-conditioned cab and a rather unusual bumper. Its partner was an American trailer. The year 1967 was the last for the CO-4000. *Ryder Truck Rentals, Oklahoma City*

An RL-700 Mack Western is waiting to be sold on return to the truck lot of Texoma Mack Sales in Denison, Texas, after the photo shoot. *Texoma Mack Sales*

This 50-inch cab International Transtar 4070 with a set of pneumatic bottom discharge bulk tank trailers was a nice combination. *Rick Manz*

One of the reefer haulers out of Chicago, Illinois, was Distributors Service Inc. Most all of their trucks were blue and white. This K-100 Kenworth was one of several running in the fleet and here it pulled a Great Dane reefer trailer. The cities served were listed on the side of the trailer. *Neil Sherff*

The "Golden Boy," as this 9500 long nose series GMC was nicknamed, was leased to the steel division of Associated Truck Lines Inc. of Grand Rapids, Michigan. A 318-horsepower Detroit Diesel engine was likely the source of power for the tri-axle steel-hauling trailer. *Neil Sherff*

This long wheelbase F-600 Mack pulled a Trailmobile reefer trailer as it trucked along the Pacific Coast. The rig was owned by Everett Higgins from Portland, Oregon. *Brian Williams*

One of the biggest for-hire common carriers was Pacific Intermountain Express Inc. of Oakland, California. When P.I.E. purchased new equipment, it was not just a few or a dozen, it was more like 200 or 300 pieces. This new White-Freightliner became part of the fleet as did the new set of Trailmobile double trailers. *P.I.E.*

The Loadstar International was the smaller version of the Fleetstar. This 1700 series belonged to the Falstaff Brewing Co. of St. Louis, Missouri. These were good trucks to be used for local pickup and delivery. The body was a Brown. *Brown Trailer Co.*

A big user of White-Freightliner trucks was Willis Shaw Frozen Express Inc. of Elm Springs, Arkansas. Shaw was a big nationwide reefer hauler with a big terminal in Idaho. A Utility reefer trailer was the partner to this tractor. *Neil Sherff*

This big truckload of furniture on sale was shipped by a W-1000 Ford and a Freuhauf furniture trailer. The truck was leased from Ryder Truck Rentals by the Lenoir Chair Co. in Lenoir, North Carolina. *Author's Collection*

E. Brooke Matlace Inc. of Lansdowne, Pennsylvania, was a big tanker hauling operation. A lot of F-600 Macks made up the tractor fleet to pull the various types of tank trailers. The company was started in 1888. *Robert Parrish*

When trucking along the East Coast on Route 1 & 9, there were many truck stops. One of the more famous ones was Scotty's Diner. The driver of this GMC 7000 thought he would give it a try. He drove for Complete Wellpoint and Equipment Corp. of Daytona Beach, Florida. He was provided with sleeping facilities for those long runs. *Harry Patterson*

Somewhat different from other rigs, this White-Freightliner tractor is pulling two trailers of two different sizes. They are hopper bottom grain trailers, brand name unknown. *Author's Collection*

Chippewa Motor Freight inc. of Eau Claire, Wisconsin, served the four states of Indiana, Illinois, Wisconsin, and Minnesota. One of the trucks that helped to serve the area was this model 7000 White and Fruehauf reefer trailer. The tractor was powered by a 220-horsepower Diesel engine. *Chippewa Motor Freight*

Jenkins Refrigerated Trucking was based in Miami, Florida, and Los Angeles, California. Owner-operators made up the fleet, like this FS-7000 Mack and Great Dane reefer trailer. The "FS" meant that the truck was made of steel components unlike the "FL" which was aluminum. The Mack Western, which was made in Hayward, California, was a popular tractor with owner-operators. *Author's Collection*

Navajo Freight lines Inc. was one of four major carriers based in Denver, Colorado. All four of them covered basically the same territory, and sadly, all four are gone into history. In this picture of the White-Freightliner tractor and Fruehauf trailer, it had the old Navajo graphics on the trailer and new graphics of the later Sixties on the tractor. Navajo became the third coast-to-coast for-hire carrier. *Robert Parrish*

Containers were usually hauled on container chassis trailers. But, it also worked to haul them on flatbed trailers like this load being pulled by a K-100 Kenworth. This long wheelbase tractor was typical of a lot of Canadian-type rigs. The company name is not quite visible but the location is New Westminster, British Columbia. *Custom Studios Ltd.*

Back in 1968, double trailers were not legal in Pennsylvania. This truck-trailer combination was actually a set of double trailers hooked together to look like a truck-trailer. Consolidated Freightways Inc. of Menlo Park, California, was one company that ran these types of trucks. The first trailer is a Comet and the second is a Brown, both being pulled by a White-Freightliner. *George Fiebe*

Another rig that belonged to Consolidated Freightways was this White-Freightliner with a true set of double Fruehauf trailers. *Consolidated Freightways*

Security Van Lines Inc. of New Orleans, Louisiana, would move just about anything. A White 7000 tractor pulled this moving van trailer. *Security Van Lines*

This owner-operator rig for Security Van Lines had dual stacks, a rare case for this White 7000 with a dromedary body. A little extra chrome added a little touch of fanciness. *Robert Parrish*

A typical western-type rig was this livestock truck-trailer combination. The White-Freightliner truck carried a Wilson livestock body and pulled a Wilson livestock pull trailer. Wilson trailers were made in Sioux City, Iowa, and were sold nationwide. *Woodworth Photos*

Dairyland's long wheelbase White-Freightliner tractor took to the road hauling milk in this tanker trailer. *Author's Collection*

The MB Mack played a role in both city delivery work and over-the-road hauling. This MB600 Mack was serving its duty for Penn Yan Express Inc. of Penn Yan, New York. With a Strick body and trailer, this truck-trailer combination was similar to those of the West, but not as long. *Author's Collection*

Crouse Transfer & Storage of Carroll, Iowa, an agent for Allied Van Lines with terminals in five Iowa cities, was the owner of this high-rise third-floor sleeper White-Freightliner tractor with a Timpte dromedary body and Timpte model TT10 trailer. *Timpte*

A big refrigerated hauler out of Denver, Colorado, was Curtis Inc. Owner-operators and small fleet operators made up the Curtis fleet. This W-900 Kenworth and reefer trailer was owned by Steinbecker Bros. of Greeley, Colorado, with main hauls of meat and meat products to the East Coast. They had a number of terminals located on the West Coast, East Coast and the Midwest. *Robert Parrish*

The GMC Astro 95 made its debut in the late Sixties. Its popularity was equal to its predecessor, the "cracker box" GMC. Imperial Co-operative Carriers based in California, had this Astro 95 pulling a Gindy trailer. *Robert Parrish*

This White 1600 was designed to haul 40-foot trailers in turnpike, inter-city operations. It was also able to pull 27-foot doubles. The source of power was a Cummins NHC-250 Diesel. This White 1600 was the prototype shown at the ATA Convention in 1969 in San Francisco. *Transport Topics*

The Mobil Oil Co. had a large fleet of trucks to deliver gasoline to their filling stations. They also had specialty trucks for certain purposes. This Fruehauf tank trailer was built to haul heavy industrial greases. The unit was insulated with fiberglass to maintain a temperature of 150 degrees to improve delivery capabilities and had its own pumping equipment. It was all pulled by a 900 series Dodge. *Mobil Oil Co.*

Miller's Transport Inc. of Hyrum, Utah, owned this model 352 Peterbilt and Wilson livestock trailer. Miller's also had a refrigerated division. The picture was taken at the port of entry in Cheyenne, Wyoming. *Harry Patterson*

The "C" model was an all-around truck that was very versatile. It could be used for small pick up and delivery, medium hauling or heavy-duty work. This model 750 straight truck with a load of General tag-a-long trailers had the optional sleeper cab. *Robert Parrish*

This RL-700 Mack Western and new Fruehauf bottom hopper dump trailer were loading up for a haul. *William Bradley Photographers*

Boise Cascade was either hauling logs from the forest to the mill or delivering the finished product. In this case, the model K-121 Kenworth hauled the finished products in a double set of Brown trailers. *Author's Collection*

John Deere Bucket Loaders were the cargo on this flatbed trailer being pulled by a Dodge tractor. The Dodge was on lease to Ringle Express Inc. of Fowler, Indiana. The picture was taken at the 76 truck stop at Bartonsville, Pennsylvania, in 1972. *Ron Adams*

Grain haulers also used truck-trailer set-ups in their operations. A White-Freightliner was the worker here, with a Wilson grain body on the back and a Wilson grain trailer tagging along. Wilson made a variety of trailers pertaining to agriculture. *Wilson Trailer Co.*

This GMC Astro 95 was teamed up with a Fruehauf four-axle dump trailer. Wildcat Trucking of Detroit, Michigan, owned the rig. *Neil Sherff*

This "A" series Autocar and Fruehauf reefer trailer for L.G. DeWitt Inc. based in Ellerbe, North Carolina, hauled refrigerated and produce cargo up the East Coast and into the Midwest. *Harry Patterson*

W.J. Digby Inc. of Denver, Colorado, was a reefer hauler to the West Coast, and drove along what is known as the Golden Arrow Route. Owner-operators were part of the Digby fleet. This FL-700 Mack Western was coupled to a Utility body chassis along with three Utility reefer bodies. These bodies could be removed and transferred onto smaller straight trucks. *Author's Collection*

In 1968, White-Freightliner came out with a first in the industry—the first extended cab. Known as the "Vanliner," it measured 104 inches and was big enough to accommodate two people. Chrome was not lacking on this tractor with four air horns, four stacks, breather bonnet, sun visor, and double bumper. The tractor and the American reefer trailer were leased on with Riss & Company of Kansas City, Missouri. *Robert Parrish*

The short nose 9500 series GMC was set up as a truck-trailer rig. Sexton Quality Foods chose a Utility body and trailer. A 6V-71 Detroit Diesel was probably the source of power to run this rig that traveled the western highways. *Author's Collection*

The new International 4070 Transtar was a slightly beefed-up version of the CO-4000. One noticeable item was a little more chrome. The late-Sixties tractor and early Fifties Brown reefer trailer was owned by Protex Industries Inc. of Denver, Colorado. *Author's Collection*

These three Fords found their way into the livestock hauling business. From left to right was the super-duty with a sleeper cab pulling a Wilson livestock trailer, a Ford 700 with a sleeper cab and livestock body, and a Ford C600 also with a livestock body. The Ford fleet owner was Leo Penry of Adkinson, Nebraska. *Author's Collection*

Livestock haulers were plentiful back in the Sixties. One of those was this International Transtar 4070 for W.J.Beachler of Loudonville, Ohio. It pulled an American livestock trailer. Not many American trailers were seen in the East. *Robert Parrish*

Transcon lines of Oklahoma City, Oklahoma, became a coast-to-coast carrier in 1965. Their authority to the East Coast came with the purchase of Kramer-Consolidated Freight Lines Inc. of Detroit, Michigan. Transcon had a White-Freightliner fleet with many Strick drop-floor trailers. *Harry Patterson*

The Mack Western came as the "FS" or "FL," and the 600 or 700. The Wescon Corp. in Corpus Christi, Texas, had this FS 700 pulling the rackside flatbed trailer. *Harry Patterson*

This Chevrolet Titan 90 and Gindy drop-floor trailer was put to work for Tenneco Chemical Co.'s general foam division in Hazelton, Pennsylvania. The Chevrolet Titan 90 and the GMC Astro 95 were basically the same truck with the same cab. *Town and Country Studios*

American Steel Inc. in Portland, Oregon, was the proud owner of this K-100 Kenworth. *Author's Collection*

The West Texas mountains and desert made a nice background for this F Model Mack and Wilson livestock trailers. These trailers had 84 feet of loading space for grown cattle and 98 feet of loading space for calves with a legal capacity of 48,000 pounds. Carter Trucking Inc. of Stratford and Amarillo, Texas, was the owner of the rig. *Author's Collection*

C&H Transportation Co. Inc. of Dallas, Texas, was a heavy hauling carrier of steel, machinery, castings, and anything that was considered heavy equipment. The fleet was made up of mostly owner-operator tractors like this F model Mack Western. C&H had a lot of nice-looking tractors in the fleet. The picture was taken at the new Flemmings truck stop at Carlisle, Pennsylvania. *Ron Adams*

Getting very good fleet fuel mileage, Frank Lumber Co. Inc. in Mill City, Oregon, ran this load of White-Freightliners efficiently. Why take wear and tear out of 54 tires when 18 will get the job done? *Author's Collection*

M&P Transport Ltd. of Ontario and Alberta, Canada, had this GMC tractor as one of their city pickup and delivery trucks. In this case a brand new Brantford trailer was being picked up at the factory. The two front and five side panels slid up and down, although its purpose remains a mystery. Notice the old-time five-digit phone number on the side of the cab. *M&P Transport Ltd.*

This R-600 Mack Western posed proudly for the camera to show off the new Alloy trailer. Puget Sound Freight Lines Inc. in Seattle, Washington, claimed proud ownership of this rig. *Puget Sound Freight Lines*

Fairchild General Freight Inc. of Yakima, Washington, had a variety of different equipment in their fleet, like this White-Freightliner with a flat dromedary body and a flatbed trailer. The company hauled a variety of commodities including fruit from orchards. *Fairchild General Freight Inc./Ken Wittmeyer Associates*

The "R" model Mack Western was a great looking truck, whether it was the 600 or the 700. Eves Trucking Co. in Phoenixville, Pennsylvania, used this RL-600 Western with a V8 Mack engine in it to pull the propane tank trailer. *Harry Patterson*

Arizona Tank Lines Inc. of Phoenix, Arizona, owned this 1970 MH9700 GMC with an 8V-71 318-horspower Detroit Diesel and Spicer 8341C transmission. The load on this truck-trailer combination was 10,000 gallons of heavy crude oil for off-highway service near Farmington, New Mexico. *Author's Collection*

This White-Freightliner tractor and its set of double outside frame flatbed trailers belonged to Clarklift. Two under-cover loads and a Clarklift hand truck were being hauled. Notice the tire chains hanging under the first trailer in case of a surprise snowstorm. *Author's Collection*

F&B Truck Lines Inc. of Slat Lake City, Utah, used this F-700 Mack Western and flatbed trailer to haul this load of venting fans for roofs. F&B covered the western states as a heavy hauler carrier. In the mid-Seventies, F&B merged with Eagle Motor Lines of Birmingham, Alabama, and became Eagle-F&B. *F&B Truck Lines Co.*

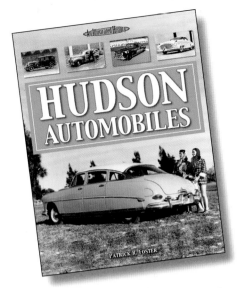

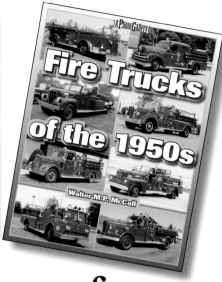

More Great Titles from Iconografix

All Iconografix books are available from specialty book dealers and bookstores worldwide, or can be ordered direct from the publisher. To request a FREE CATALOG or to place an order contact:

Iconografix
Dept BK
1830A Hanley Road
Hudson, WI 54016

Call:
(800) 289-3504
715-381-9755

Email: info@iconobooks.com

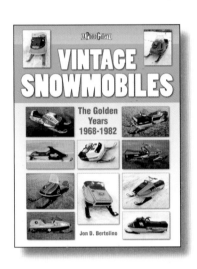

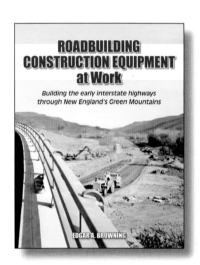

To see our complete selection of over 7,000 titles, visit us at:
www.enthusiastbooks.com
We would love to hear from you!

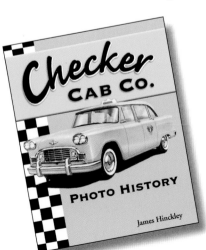

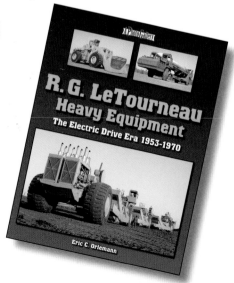